# Stories from Big Pine Lake

Jerome B. Imhoff

outskirts
press

STORIES FROM BIG PINE LAKE

By: Jerome B. Imhoff

The Ice Rescue
Edward and the January Thaw
The Great Beaver Pond Flood
The Deer Mouse House
Uncle Bert and the Almost Two Mile Hike
Edward and the Va Room Ba Doom
The Spring Peepers
The Whoosh!

# TABLE OF CONTENTS

# FOREWORD

The Ice Rescue is a true story. It happened on Hitchcock Lake in Waterbury, Connecticut around 1973. It was witnessed by James McCarthy, a long time resident of the lake. The story was relayed to me by Mr. McCarthy's nephew, Jack Rourke in 1987.

The other stories in this collection are fictional. The location and environs however, are real. The stories take place on and around Crescent Lake in Enfield, Connecticut. The animals used in the stories are real, just like The High Meadow, The Bull Frog Bog, The Great Road (State Rd. 220), The Beaver Dam and Lodge, the Deep Woods, and the Railroad Tracks. J. Duncan Beaver lived part time under my lake garden in the early and mid 1990's. The woodchuck colony did indeed live on the High Meadow, above The Great Road . The property belongs to the State of Connecticut Department of Correction, for whom I worked for nearly 24 years. My proximity to their environs gave me a unique opportunity to study the habits of the animals throughout the year, going into and out of hibernation.

I became familiar with the sights and sounds of the lake at close range, a privilege granted to only a few. My dock and my canoe were my observation posts and the world of natural things unfolded before my eyes on a daily basis. There I learned to appreciate the small creatures and events in their lives that are overlooked by most people. Enjoy the stories. J.B. Imhoff

# SYNOPSIS

Big Pine Lake is really Crescent Lake in Enfield, Connecticut. The family of woodchucks lived on the High Meadow overlooking the lake. The places identified in the stories and the animals are real. The animals that frequented the lake were regular guests in my back yard and were a constant source of amazement.

My young son used to wait every spring and every fall for the return of the Canada Geese. He would stand at the end of our dock with his bag of cracked corn, waving and calling, "Welcome back geese!" and they would swim to him, tentatively at first, to be fed. J. Duncan Beaver lived on the quiet cove and under our lake garden timbers in two very cozy lodges. The Great Beaver Pond Flood was a real event.

Edward is modeled after my younger brother Ed, now retired. He is a curious and kind man, also a wonderful fiction writer who is now a naturally bearded Santa Clause living in Wichita Kansas.

Uncle Bert is our late Uncle Bert Bremmer who knew every backwater pond and fishing hole on the lower Wisconsin River. The spring peepers were our first real sign of spring in the north and we waited all winter to hear them calling into the night in early April when we were kids.

Gustav and Gerte were our great aunt and uncle in Wisconsin, both loyal and kind. The Ice Rescue is dedicated to them and to the migrating flock of geese that would come every spring and every fall on their way to and from their winter home on the Chesapeake Bay.

We were lucky to be able to watch animals in their own environs at close range, both in Wisconsin as a young man and in Connecticut as an adult. It taught us to appreciate them and to cherish each moment and each shared adventure.

# THE ICE RESCUE

The blustery December wind, the plunging temperature and the first clear layer of ice signaled the beginning of winter on Big Pine Lake. The shore cottages stood silent with their windows and doors boarded up for the winter. The children who swam and sailed on the lake in summer had long since gone back to their schools in the city. All that remained were the creatures that lived in the woods along the shore or on what little water the Canada geese were able to keep open during the long winter months.

The wintering geese had been stirring quietly on the open patch of water through the night but something was dreadfully wrong. Girte, one of the oldest geese in the flock had arrived very tired and very late in the night and had settled in on the far edge of the open water. She had nestled her head into the long soft feathers of her back and had fallen quickly asleep. She was awakened by the thin, sharp rays of the cold morning sun and the squawking of three-hundred-fifty-four frantic geese. With necks straining, they honked as loudly as they could, "Girte, wake up! Wake up! You'll die if you don't move!"

Girte could feel the ice beginning to squeeze in around her. She looked quickly around and she too became frantic. Though she could move her feet, her wings were frozen solid into the smooth, hard surface of the lake. Soon the geese began to climb up onto the ice. With their wings flapping, they slipped and slid as they tried to run from the open water to where Girte was stuck in the ice. Everyone wanted to help but none of the worried geese knew what to do.

None of the geese had ever seen such a dilemma, none that is except Gustav, the oldest and wisest goose in the flock. He had seen other geese stuck in the ice in years past and knew the danger all too well. While the other geese squawked and flapped about Girte, Gustav looked carefully around, checking for anything else that could hurt her.

To the north, the gray storm clouds were beginning to form. By nightfall it would surely be snowing. That worried Gustav but what he saw next sent shivers down the feathers of his long, gray back. In the woods that came nearly to the frozen waters edge, the greatest danger of all, peered intently from behind the tree line. Dred, the red fox was waiting patiently for nightfall. The fall had been especially cold and food was particularly scarce for this time of year. A goose, frozen in the ice was easy prey and would be a fine supper for a hungry fox family.

That was all Gustav had to see. He knew then and there, just what had to be done. With powerful strokes from his long graceful wings, he skimmed over the small patch of open water into the air, quickly circling the flock. Below him the frantic geese had begun pecking at the ice around Girte with their bills but the ice had become too thick during the night. She was still trapped unable to move and she was too worried to notice the storm clouds or Dred the red fox.

As he circled the flock, Gustav honked loudly to the others. It was difficult to be heard over the noise of so many frightened, squawking geese so he flew low over them, flapping his wings wildly and honking as loud as he could. The flock finally took notice of Gustav and suddenly the lake was silent. They knew him to be old and wise and they listened carefully, hoping he could help them rescue Girte.

Now that the flock was quiet, Gustav circled quickly and landed in the water near the edge of the ice, swimming as close to Girte as he could. The distance between Girte and the open water seemed so very long. They must hurry or it would be too late. It would take all of them and they would have only one chance to rescue her.

The sun was now shining brightly on the open patch of water, warming the surface ever so slightly as Gustav dipped his giant wings into the lake. He pushed the water against the ice in the direction of his trapped friend. The other geese watched in amazement. The motion of the sun warmed water had begun to wear a path in the ice toward Girte but Gustav's wings were becoming very tired. He was working so hard, he hadn't noticed the younger, stronger geese lining up behind him. When he stopped to rest, the younger geese moved into position, each goose taking his turn lapping the water up against the ice. The rescue was actually working!

Dred, the red fox, watched curiously as this strange parade of geese worked through the day to free Girte, who had struggled so long and so hard that her long neck fell limp and her head lay exhausted on the ice. There would however, be no goose dinner for the foxes that night. As the afternoon came to an end, the sun disappeared behind the heavy, approaching storm clouds and the geese were very near to Girte with their rescue path. As the water pushers worked with their long, strong wings, others swam back and forth in the channel they had created in order to keep the water from freezing once again into ice.

Darkness came to the gray sky and the large, soft flakes of snow had begun to fall on the ice as the water pushers finally reached Girte. With tired wings they worked their way around her as Gustav carefully freed her long, gray flight feathers from the ice. Finally Girte broke free from the icy grip and with Gustav in the lead she swam down the opened water channel to the joyfully squawking flock in the center of the patch of open water.

As the soft, early December snow fell on the mostly frozen lake, Girte swam to each of the water pushers and gently rubbed her long neck over their tired wings. Then she swam close to Gustav in the middle of the flock, nestled her head once again into the long, soft feathers of her back and with a deep sigh, drifted off to sleep.

**THE END**

# EDWARD AND THE
# JANUARY THAW

Winter had come to the High Meadow overlooking Big Pine Lake. Snow swirled with the biting north wind and covered the hillside. Deep in his burrow Edward slept on his bed made of soft marsh grass and dreamed of last summer, of playing hide and seek in the High Meadow clover and watching the men in yellow hats who had repaired the Great Road.

Edward and the rest of the woodchucks had been asleep for nearly two months, deep in their burrows beneath the High Meadow but in late January something unusual happened. One morning the temperature began to rise. Water started dripping from the melting snow, down into the burrows and Edward woke up, stretched his short arms and legs and thought about lunch. Edward thought about lunch,............a lot!

The January thaw had come to the High Meadow, just warm enough to melt some of the snow and wake the hibernating animals for only a few short days before the bitter cold and snow of winter returned. Edward thought "it must be spring." He poked his nose out into the tunnel that led up to the Look-Out Rock and checked to see if any of his friends were awake yet.

When he reached the top of the tunnel he couldn't believe his eyes. Just like in spring, there was bright sun that warmed his thick brown fur and melted the snow from on top of the Look-Out Rock. Just like in spring, he could feel the freshness in the air and he could hear birds singing. This was exciting! It must be Spring!

But.........There were no tender green shoots of spring grass and there were no bees or dragon flies buzzing about. Instead, the bright sun hurt his eyes at first as it glared off the thick blanket of snow that stretched beyond the Great Road and far past Big Pine Lake. The snow covered everything as far as Edward could see. This was very exciting and he wanted very much for it to be spring but it wasn't spring, not yet.

Edward did not want to be excited alone because this looked like it could be fun. He bounced down from the Look-Out Rock and scurried back down into the dark tunnel, past his door and into the next tunnel. He knocked on each door and as his neighbors poked their noses out, they could hear Edward. "Come quick! Come quick! I think it's spring! I think it's spring! It must be time to play."

The other woodchucks, still a little sleepy, popped out of their burrows and climbed up into the bright sun. Almost everyone thought it was spring, except for Uncle Bert who was the last one out of the burrow. His fur was old and a little thin so he had put on his checkered cap, cocked off to one side just a little, and a long, red muffler because He knew from experience that it wasn't really spring. It was however, time to have some fun, if only or a day or two.

All the woodchucks looked curiously at Uncle Bert. In his paws he carried a shiny tin pie plate with a long piece of string from an old hay bale attached to one side. He tapped on the pie plate like a drum to get the attention of the waiting, curious woodchucks. Ears perked up and everyone listened carefully. "Don't be fooled." he began. "This isn't really spring, even though it feels warm. It's just the January Thaw. It happens almost every year at this time of winter and only lasts for a few short days. It will be very cold again soon but for a little while, we can have some real fun!"

None of the younger woodchucks had ever seen winter before so they wondered what kind of fun they could have with snow. It was cold and flat and there was so much of it. They watched in wonder as Uncle Bert trudged to the top of the hill overlooking the High Meadow, dragging the tin pie plate at the end of the string.

When he reached the top, he put the shiny tin pie plate down flat on the snow. Very carefully he put the string between his teeth, stepped gingerly onto the pie plate and sat down, Ker-Plop! Now that was a sight, Uncle Bert with the string in his mouth, sitting in the tin pie plate on top of the hill in the snow. What on earth was he doing?

Just when everyone was wondering, just that, Uncle Bert turned his cap around, tightened his long red muffler and pushed off with his front paws. Down the hill he slid, spinning and shouting "Whee! Whee! Whoopie!" bouncing and bumping, spinning and whirling until he came to a stop with a sodden thump, right in the middle of a snow drift.

In an instant, the rest of the woodchucks knew what the January Thaw was all about. Into their burrows they raced, grabbing anything they could find that was flat and would slide; pots and pans and shoebox lids, became sleds and saucers speeding across the snow. The hill from the High Meadow became a winter playground like the woodchucks had never seen.

Uncle Bert got tired first. He climbed up on the Look-Out Rock to watch the activity on the hill. He remembered the January thaws when he was young, the worn out water ski toboggan he had made and the fun they had for just a few days each January. It was a happy time for Uncle Bert to remember. He remembered the snowmen, the excitement and being young once again.

This year the January thaw was longer than usual and lasted almost a whole week. Everyone got to play in the snow. On Saturday Uncle Bert called Edward up to the Look-Out Rock and pointed to the western sky. The dark gray storm clouds were gathering and the wind began to bite at their faces as it blew across the High Meadow. "Best call everyone in Edward. The storm is coming in fast. By morning, the High Meadow will have a new deep blanket of snow and it will be very cold once again."

Edward called and one by one, the woodchucks slid down the hill for one last time and slipped into their burrows. They put away their pots and pans and shoe box sleds and hung up their mittens and mufflers. When Edward went to check on Uncle Bert, he was already sound asleep with his long red muffler wrapped snugly around his neck and his cap cocked off to one side, just a little.

Edward smiled and covered Uncle Bert with his warm marsh grass quilt. Then he returned to his own burrow, put the straw cover over his doorway, poured a cup of dried sweet clover tea and slid gingerly into his own warm bed and fell fast asleep, to dream about high adventure, tin pan sleds, snow slides and the January Thaw.

## THE END

# THE GREAT BEAVER POND FLOOD

Everything around Big Pine Lake had come alive. It was truly spring at last. The winter had been long and cold and everyone felt better in the warm fresh breeze on the High Meadow. Andrew the fish-hawk soared high in the warm updraft, watching all the activity below.

The woodchucks were busy gathering spring violets and fresh white clover on the High Meadow. Douglas the deer-mouse was getting used to his new home up on Nob Hill and as evening drew near, the spring peepers sang to their hearts content on the edge of the Bull Frog Bog. All looked and felt much like it should. After all, this was Spring!

J. Duncan Beaver was looking over his lodgings and the dam he had built last fall, to separate the pond from Big Pine Lake. He flipped his tail from side to side as he swam back and forth rearranging braces and sticks that had loosened up during the winter shifting of ice.

He looked at his handiwork and thought to himself, "Very fine work, very fine indeed."

As the peepers sang their last songs of the evening, a gentle rain began to fall. J. Duncan Beaver slid silently beneath the water with one quick flash of his tail and slipped into the underwater entrance to his lodge. Inside it was warm and cozy and so quiet that he couldn't hear the rain coming down harder and harder.

All through the night it stormed and on into the next morning as well. Andrew stood silently at the entrance to his home in the hole of the hollow pine tree. It was raining much too hard for him to fly. He could only watch as the wind howled and blew the rain in great sheets across Big Pine Lake.

Peter the muskrat looked around, first to the right toward the Bull Frog Bog and then to the left toward the Beaver Pond. The beaver dam was holding just fine. J. Duncan Beaver had built it well but the water in the pond was rising rapidly, too rapidly.

Peter swam quickly to the carefully constructed beaver dam and climbed up on top to take a closer look. He looked toward the beaver lodge just in time to see the very top of it disappear beneath the water. Peter knew that this meant trouble. The air vent for the beaver lodge was now under water. J. Duncan Beaver would surely be trapped if his ceiling turned to mud and caved in.

Peter slipped quickly back into the water and swam toward where the top of the beaver lodge had been. He dove down to find the underwater entrance but got confused by the sticks and willow branches that covered it. The round sides of the beaver lodge all looked the same from under the water. Again and again he dove down and swam around searching for the entrance. Finally, when he was nearly ready to give up, he found it!

Peter squeezed into the entrance and up into the tunnel that led to the hollow inside the lodge. J. Duncan Beaver was curled up in the warm corner of the hollow, fast asleep. Peter knew it would not be safe inside for long, with water over the top of the lodge. He ran to the corner and began to shake J. Duncan Beaver's shoulder. "J. Duncan, wake up! Please wake up!" shouted Peter.

Drops of water were beginning to fall from the ceiling inside the beaver lodge and the air was getting musty and thin. J. Duncan Beaver sat up, shook himself and wondered for just a moment, what Peter was doing in his house, jumping up and down frantically. "Hurry, J. Duncan! We must get out of here, NOW! The tunnel will cave in and we'll both be trapped."

It took a minute but J. Duncan Beaver finally understood what Peter was all excited about. The roof of the tunnel was turning into mud and there was barely enough room for them to squeeze through the tunnel but they made it to the entrance safely. They had gotten out, just in time.

They swam to the beaver dam and climbed up on top. They would need to make a hole in the dam to lower the water on the beaver pond. J. Duncan Beaver dove to the bottom and began loosening the carefully placed sticks and willow branches. Peter pulled them from the top and little by little the dam began to open up. Peter and J. Duncan Beaver sat silently in the pouring rain, watching the water push through the now gaping hole in the dam and down into Big Pine Lake. His house was gone and his dam had a huge hole in it. J.

Duncan Beaver thought about all the hard work he had done and became very sad.

After two days it finally stopped raining and the caved in top of the beaver lodge appeared above the water. Andrew the fish-hawk was glad the rain had stopped too because he was getting very hungry. He stretched his graceful wings out wide and soared over the lake. He would tell the other animals about the beaver pond flood.

By early the next morning, the whole countryside was abuzz. Everyone had heard about the flood. One by one, the animals came to help J. Duncan Beaver. The striped skunk brought a bundle of willow branches to help mend the dam. Edward and Uncle Bert brought spring violets and other sweet morsels from the High Meadow to help feed the workers and the porcupine from the Deep Woods brought mushrooms for mushroom stew. They all pitched in to help rebuild the beaver lodge, each in his own way.

By weeks end, a fine new beaver lodge stood in the middle of the pond. J. Duncan Beaver served mushroom stew and thanked each of his friends. That night, they all sat around the fire at the edge of the pond, listening to the songs of the spring peepers and telling stories, and talking quietly about the spring rains and the Great Beaver Pond Flood.

**THE END**

D.M.H

# THE DEER MOUSE HOUSE

After a long, cold winter, it was finally spring and Edward knew that meant rain on the High Meadow. He knew the rain would wash the winter dirt from his fur and would help the seeds in the ground turn into tasty sweet-clover. Ordinarily he liked the rain but today the sky looked dark and threatening. He sat uneasily on top of the Look-Out Rock and watched the dark storm clouds roll and rumble through the sky over Big Pine Lake.

Suddenly he felt a strange damp chill in the air. Birds of every size and color came bursting through the trees at the edge of the Deep Woods as though they were being chased by something. He heard the rumbling, roaring sound of the wind as it grew stronger and louder. He could feel the fur stand straight out on the back of his neck and he began to tremble.

The wind howled as it burst through the trees. Leaves and dead branches hurtled into the air as the wind churned wildly toward the Great Road. Then suddenly it turned, heading straight up the hill toward the High Meadow. The long, dark, twisting cloud was headed straight toward him.

Woodchucks went scurrying into the safety of their burrows. The white tail deer ran pell-mell, bounding over fence rows and through thick bushy-brush to escape the wind. Edward just stood there, shaking with fear, as if frozen beside the Look-Out Rock. In the dark cloud filled with wind, he could see birds and boards and bushel baskets sailing through the air as if flung by a whirling giant.

Just in the nick of time. Uncle Bert popped out of his burrow, grabbed Edward's leg and pulled him quickly down to safety. Outside, the wind roared and howled as it raced over the High Meadow. Edward and Uncle Bert listened for what seemed a very long time, until the awful howl of the wind was gone, as suddenly as it had come. Uncle Bert said, "Must have been a tornado" and sure enough, it was but tornadoes come and go quickly and soon the air was still, very still indeed.

Ever so slowly, Edward crept out of the burrow, smelling, looking and listening very carefully to be sure the tornado was gone and it was safe to go outside once again. The wind was gone and everything was quiet. There were no birds, no bees, and no butterflies, no, not even one. All he could hear was the silence left by the wind. There were branches and broken boards, sign posts and shingles strewn all around the High Meadow. The wind had carried everything imaginable and dropped it helter-skelter all the way down to the great Road.

Edward looked out across the meadow from the Look-Out Rock when he heard the sound of chattering teeth. "Chitter-Chitter. Chit, Chit. Chit. The old wooden sign on top of the Look-Out rock had been blown away but still clinging to the marker post was a small brown deer mouse. His little brown nose, ears too big for his head and mousey brown fur were all rumpled and wet from the wind and rain. His eyes were still tightly shut as he clung there to the post, still afraid to move or to look. He just trembled and chattered with fear.

Edward just sat and watched for a moment, still a little scared himself and curious to know how the deer mouse had come to the Look-Out Rock.

The deer mouse finally opened his eyes, just a little and looked warily around. He looked up at Edward, who stood much taller than a deer mouse and jumped back quickly. What was this huge, furry creature with beady brown eyes and teeny-tiny ears? Then Edward leaned down, reached out his paw and lifted the fright-ened mouse up to his eye level. He looked into the deer mouse's eyes and said, "Hullow, I'm Edward and who might you be?"

The mouse was so relieved to think that Edward wasn't going to eat him that he blurted out. all in one breath. "I'm Douglas the deer mouse and I live on the far side of the Deep Woods and I got picked up by the wind...and I want to go home!" Not only was Douglas relieved to have survived the tornado, but he was most relieved that woodchucks didn't eat mice. Douglas was only sure of two things. He was far from home and his home, was probably destroyed by the tornado and was gone.

Edward however, was already thinking. "Wait here." he said. "I think I have an idea!" Douglas waited nervously as Edward popped into the tunnel that led to Uncle Bert's burrow. "The map. Uncle Bert, where's the map? Can I borrow the map?" Uncle Bert reached high on the shelf for the tightly rolled, very old map and handed it to Edward. In no time flat, Edward scurried out of Uncle Bert's burrow, up through the tunnel and was carefully spreading the well worn map out on the grass next to the Look-Out Rock.

Douglas looked down curiously from his perch on the empty sign post. It looked like a very long way from the High Meadow to anywhere else on the map, Especially in deer mouse steps. Douglas knew that he couldn't go back to his old house on the far side of the Deep Woods because the tornado had blown it away. It was hard for him to hold back the tears. He just wanted to go home.

Edward poured over the old map in search of a new home for Douglas. There was the Bull Frog Bog but that was too swampy. There was Turtle Cove but that was too far. He thought about the Raspberry Patch but there were too many prickers and there were other places in the Deep Forest but none seemed just right for a deer-mouse house.

About that time, Uncle Bert lumbered out of the tunnel into the afternoon sunlight. "How goes the search?" he said to Edward, "and who's your young friend?" "This is Douglas the deer mouse. He was blown here by the tornado. The search isn't going so well. Everything is either too far or too wet or just not quite right. Will you help us, please?"

Uncle Bert sat down, looked over the map and thought long and hard. He looked out over the High Meadow and on toward the Deep Woods. The woodland animals were starting to move around, checking their homes and their neighbors after the tornado. Just then, Roger the fish eagle glided overhead, carried aloft by the warm updraft beyond the High Meadow and on toward Nob Hill.

"That's it!" sad Uncle Bert. Nob Hill! If the wind hasn't torn it up too badly, it would be a perfect home for a deer mouse. There are bushes for berries and shade and there are three small burrows, left by the ground squirrels who lived there two summer's ago. Let's go have us a look." Douglas climbed up on Uncle Bert's shoulder and Edward bounded along beside, and they were on their way to Nob Hill.

When they reached the top of Nob Hill, they found the shade bushes with ripe red berries, unharmed by the tornado. They found the three small burrows left by the ground squirrels, still empty. As they cleared the hilltop of boards and bags and shingles, carried there by the wind, Douglas found the most precious treasure of all. On a familiar old small board sign, thrown afar by the tornado, were familiar words in simple black print.

Uncle Bert found a stick to use as a post and Douglas found a stone and two bent nails from an old sign while Edward built a small cooking fire on which to make a sweet clover salad for supper. The fire crackled long into the night with shadows of the three furry shapes visible only from close up as they sat and told tall tales under the old wind blown sign that read: Deer Mouse House - Welcome.

THE END

Whoosh!
Whoosh!

# UNCLE BERT AND THE ALMOST TWO MILE HIKE

Finally, spring had come to the High Meadow and Edward had finished cleaning and airing out his burrow after the long winter's hibernation. He and his Uncle Bert were sitting next to the Look-Out Rock nibbling on violet stems and spring clover blossoms. High above, glided Andrew the old fish hawk, enjoying the warmth of the spring breeze under his wings as it lifted him higher and higher into the sky.

"I wish I could go where Andrew goes and see all the things he sees." Edward said earnestly. Uncle Bert looked kindly at him, so young and full of wonder. He remembered the spring after his first winter's hibernation and how curious he was about places beyond the High Meadow. Then, all at once, he had an idea! In the blink of an eye. Uncle Bert popped out of sight, down into the tunnel leading to his burrow. On top of the shelf in the corner of his burrow was an old worn and dog-eared map. It hadn't been used in many years but he had a feeling that he'd put it to use very soon. When he poked his nose out of the burrow again, there was Edward, now standing on top of the Look-Out Rock, squinting to see Andrew, gliding far off into the distance.

"Edward" said Uncle Bert, "Let's take a hike down by Big Pine Lake." Uncle Bert had carefully unfolded the map and Edward was getting excited at the prospect of an adventure. Woodchucks like adventures, you know. There on the ground was a picture of what Andrew the fish Hawk must have seen as he soared over the High Meadow. There was the long tunnel under The Great Road, paved by the men in yellow hats. Beyond the Great Road was the potato field, the Bull Frog Bog, the Slippery Stream and the Beaver Pond. Far in the distance, at the end of the lake and almost a mile from the High Meadow was the Pine Forest and the railroad bridge over Turtle Cove.

There were lots of names on the map, like Fox Den - "Be Careful", and Beaver Lodge - home of J. Duncan Beaver and Raspberry Patch- "prickers," underwater stumps, pheasant trees and Turtle Cove. The trail was clearly marked and Edward was clearly ready. So, with hiking sticks in hand and red bandanas around their necks, Edward and Uncle Bert set out on their almost two mile hike. Now it's important to remember that two miles to a growing child isn't too far but for a woodchuck with short, squat legs, it can be a very long walk indeed.

The first leg of their journey went by quickly. Without saying anything to Uncle Bert, Edward thought to himself, "This hiking is quite easy." Uncle Bert was thinking too. "I hope Edward realizes it's easy here because it's all down hill." Edward of course, didn't. He just bounced down the hill from the High Meadow on the Clearly Marked Trail, happy to be off on his first adventure with Uncle Bert.

At the bottom of the hill was the Great Road, paved last summer by the men in yellow hats. It looked long and straight and cars whizzed by......Whoosh! A red Whoosh then Whoosh! A blue Whoosh, Whoosh!...... Whoosh! Edward stopped to watch the passing cars while Uncle Bert wiped his brow with his red bandana. "We had best use the cement tunnel under the road." said Uncle Bert. "It's much safer than crossing over the top."

The tunnel was long and cool and a little wet at the bottom but they could see the sunlight at the other end so they scurried on through, Edward pretending of course, not to be afraid. At the end of the tunnel they jumped down, back onto the clearly marked trail that ran along the edge of the potato field, through the raspberry patch and on toward the Bull Frog Bog. When they reached the Bull Frog Bog, Uncle Bert needed to rest again so he took a long, cool drink of water and sat down with a thump! on top of an old cedar stump, probably left there by the tree cutters, just for resting. Uncle Bert tried to get Edward to sit for a spell and listen for the spring sounds on the bog but Edward wanted to explore. He stopped just long enough to take a quick sip of water and then bounded off in the direction of the Slippery Stream.

It was getting on toward mid-day when Edward and Uncle Bert reached the Slippery Stream. Without looking at the thin green grass, waving back and forth under the water, Edward stepped on a log at the water's edge, lost his balance, dropped his hiking stick and went sliding feet first, down the Slippery' Stream, over the smooth rounded rocks, under the willow tree and right past Uncle Bert. He finally came to rest with a not so graceful SPLASH!, smack dab under the crooked sign that read, "NO SWIMMING."

Uncle Bert couldn't help but chuckle to himself as he reached out with his hiking stick while hanging very tightly onto a willow branch. Edward grabbed the end of the stick and Uncle Bert pulled him safely ashore. Edward found a sunny spot on a flat rock, shook himself off soundly, making the water spray in every direction. The warm breeze felt good as it moved through his wet fur. Andrew the fish hawk glided over, looked down at Edward and called. "Everything all right down there?" Edward squinted into the sun and waved as Andrew flew on in the direction of Turtle Cove.

Once Edward was dry, they continued on. The warmest part of the afternoon was spent in the shade of the tall pine forest. The bark of the pine trees was sticky with spring sap and the emerald green needles filled the air with the smell of new growth. It was almost supper time when Edward and Uncle Bert left the shade of the pine forest and climbed up onto the long railroad bridge that crossed Turtle Cove. Edward was starving so Uncle Bert reached deep into his jacket pocket and pulled out two bags of almost fresh violet stems. They munched happily, sitting side by side on the steel train track, watching the turtle heads popping up to catch bugs on the surface of the water.

Suddenly Uncle Bert felt something. It was a strange vibration coming through his fur. "Edward." he said. "I think we better get off this bridge. That vibration means

A TRAIN IS COMING!" Hiking sticks flew one way and violet stems flew another as Edward and Uncle Bert dashed frantically toward the far end of the bridge. By now they could see the train and hear the rumble of its huge steel wheels but woodchucks are so small, that the engineer couldn't see THEM.

Edward, Uncle Bert and the train all reached the end of the bridge at about the same time. Uncle Bert grabbed Edward's arm and yelled "JUMP!!!" Clickety clack, Whoosh! Whoosh! Clickety clack Whoosh! Clickety clack, clickety clack, clack, clack, clack, clack.........Then, just as suddenly as it had come, the train was gone, on down the track toward Cottage Grove, Sun Prairie and points beyond. Edward and Uncle Bert were busy catching their breath, retrieving their hiking sticks and trying to collect their wits. Their short legs were not well suited for outrunning trains.

The sun was beginning to go down and Uncle Bert knew they were still some distance from the Beaver Pond, the home of his friend. J. Duncan Beaver. He knew they would have to spend the night in his beaver lodge because they were still almost a mile from their burrows on the High Meadow and they would never make it home before dark.

Off in the distance. Uncle Bert saw the den of Dred the red fox. He hoped that the fox wasn't out hunting yet. He didn't want them to become supper for a hungry fox family. Quickly they moved along the shore of Big Pine Lake toward the Beaver Pond. As they passed through the swamp oak grove, they saw the dark shapes of pheasants on their night perches in the low branches of the trees, just beyond the reach of the hunting fox. They were relieved when the pheasants called to them.

"You're safe now. The coast is clear." We'll fly over and let J. Duncan Beaver know you're coming."

J. Duncan Beaver was waiting on the edge of the Beaver Pond as Uncle Bert and Edward came out of the Oak Grove. "Welcome friends" he called. The pheasants told me to expect guests for the night. Uncle Bert was relieved to hear his old friend's voice and was glad to see the waiting raft that floated them to the safety of the beaver lodge in the middle of the pond. There was a cooking pot over the fire with a fine supper of cat-tail stew and fresh spring iris roots. It was a fine feast indeed after the adventure of the hike.

The fire crackled long into the night. Uncle Bert and J. Duncan Beaver sat in the glow of the fire telling stories of hikes and hawks and listening to the night sounds of the bull frogs on Big Pine Lake. Edward stayed awake as long as he could but after a big bowl of cat-tail stew and two cups of iris root tea. he fell fast asleep on a nest of soft pine boughs, to dream of the days adventures with Uncle Bert on their almost two mile hike.

THE END

Va Room!
Ba Doom!

# EDWARD AND THE VA ROOM BA DOOM

Spring had finally come to the hills overlooking Big Pine Lake and once again the sun warmed the ground on the High Meadow. Deep inside his burrow, where he had slept through the long, cold winter, a young woodchuck named Edward began to stir.

The snow had melted with the warm breeze and the chirping sounds of the first robins drifted into the burrows. The High Meadow above the Great Road was coming alive. Soon the entire colony of woodchucks would be abuzz with activity. Deep in his burrow beneath the Look-Out Rock, Edward was rustling about. He carefully checked the pots of seeds and small roots that he would need for food until the spring rains brought new growth to the grass and wildflowers on the High Meadow.

After five long months of hibernation, Edward was anxious to go outside. He tugged at the thatch door cover that protected his burrow from the swirling winter wind. Sunlight from above was already warming the tunnel. Timidly at first, he poked his nose out into the fresh, clean spring air. The gentle breeze felt good as it rustled his thick, warm winter fur.

Ever so cautiously he poked his head out of the burrow, smelling the air and listening very carefully. This was Edward's second spring and he didn't want to miss a thing. From the top of the Look-Out Rock he could see the Canada Geese resting on Big Pine Lake. Through the trees he saw the den of Dred, the red fox and the sleeping thickets of the white tail deer.

It all looked just like he thought it should until he looked far down the Great Road that ran past the High Meadow. Far in the distance he could see men in yellow hats, one with a long, striped stick and one with a looking glass on legs. Edward wondered what the men were doing on the old bumpy, curvy road. Woodchucks can be quite curious, you know. He thought he had better find out.

All that day he went from burrow to burrow, asking the older members of the colony about the men in yellow hats. He was so excited that he could hardly contain himself but none of the older woodchucks had ever seen the men in yellow hats before. They told Edward, "the men will probably be gone by morning, not to worry. Let's find something to eat." Woodchucks, you know, are always hungry. Even though the workmen were gone by the end of the day, Edward was still excited and curious as he curled up in his burrow for the night on his bed of dried marsh hay.

But in the morning, Edward was shaken awake by a strange rumbling sound, far in the distance, Va Room Ba Doom, Va Room Ba Doom, Ba Doom Ba Doom, Ba

Doom! He could feel it coming closer and closer and closer.

By now, all the woodchucks were thumping and bumping as they scurried frantically through their burrows and tunnels beneath the High Meadow. Inside, Edward's burrow the walls were trembling and dirt crumbs were falling from the roof like rain drops. Edward gathered his courage and scrambled through the doorway and up the tunnel to the Look-Out Rock. Now the Great winding Road was crowded with men in yellow hats. Some had shovels. Some were in big green dump trucks and one held a red sign that said "STOP!"

He could see great earth movers that pushed the ground from one place to another. There were back hoes with giant scoops, graders that made the rough ground flat and then there it was, the Va Room Ba Doom that rolled over the ground and stones, making everything shake.

Edward watched the man with the striped stick. Now he was much closer than yesterday. He was coming closer and closer to the High Meadow, moving the stick from place to place and waving to the man with a looking glass on legs. Edward began to worry that the men in yellow hats were not there just to fix the road. He needed to find out for sure. With all the courage he could pack into his round, brown, furry body, Edward climbed down the Look-Out Rock and scurried down the clearly marked trail toward the man with the looking glass on legs.

The man saw him coming. "Good morning Mr. Woodchuck," he called as Edward approached. The man bent down to get a closer look at his by now, very curious visitor. Edward stopped quickly to take a long and careful look at the man before getting any closer. He looked straight into the eyes of the man with the looking glass on legs and announced, "I'm Edward and something is shaking the walls and roofs of our burrows up on the High Meadow. We are afraid of the Va Room Ba Doom. Please make it go away!"

The man with the looking glass on legs looked earnestly at Edward and said, "My name is Mr. Casey and I can't make them stop but I can show you what they are doing and what made the ground shake your burrows. Climb up on my shoulder and we'll take a closer look." Edward was as much afraid as he was curious. He had never been this close to a real person before. Mr. Casey held out his arm and Edward hung on tight as he swung up and perched precariously on Mr. Casey's shoulder, right next to his bright yellow hat.

Coming down the road he heard the loud, rumbling sound again. Edward stood as tall as his short, squat legs would allow. He hung on tight and peered over the top of Mr. Casey's yellow hat. Mr. Casey could feel Edward trembling as the Va Room Ba Doom suddenly stopped. "Don't be afraid Edward" said Mr. Casey. "It's only the road roller and it only rumbles and shakes the ground when it rolls over rocks and stones and gravel. It is very heavy and filled with water and can make an awful noise but when it makes the road smooth, the roller will become quiet again. When the dump trucks bring the new blacktop, you'll see. The roller will be very quiet and it won't shake your burrows any more."

"You see Edward, there were too many dangerous curves and pot holes on this road. In winter, while you were asleep in your burrow, ice would form on the curves and it would be too slippery to drive on. Fire trucks could not reach the houses on Big Pine Lake and people were getting hurt when their cars slid off the road."

Now Edward understood about the men in yellow hats, the big green dump trucks and the noise of the Va Room Ba Doom. He was anxious to tell the other woodchucks the news so they would no longer be afraid. He thanked Mr. Casey as he lowered him gently to the ground, then scurried between the wooden legs that held the looking glass and scrambled up the clearly marked trail to the High Meadow.

All the other woodchucks had gathered at the top of the High Meadow near the Look-Out Rock, stretching to see and waiting not very patiently to hear the news. The grandparents wondered and pulled quietly on their gray whiskers. The parents wondered and chattered with excitement, watching the young woodchucks carefully so they didn't play too close to the edge of the High Meadow.

Edward was very excited and completely out of breath when he reached the High Meadow. Running up-hill was much more work than running down the Clearly Marked Trail. When he caught his breath, he told the others about the men in the yellow hats, about Mr. Casey and the Va Room Ba Doom that made everything smooth. They were all proud of Edward for being brave and talking to Mr. Casey. This had been a lot of excitement for so early in the year and they were all relieved.

The woodchucks watched from the High Meadow through the spring and into the summer as the Great Road was straightened and paved and they watched Mr. Casey wave as the Va Room Ba Doom finally rolled away, this time, very quietly.

The Great Road was now smooth and safe for the fire trucks and cars. There were no big green dump trucks and no earth movers, no men in yellow hats and no more Va Room Ba Doom. It was time to do what woodchucks do best, munch on sweet clover, listen to the birds sing and the honey bees buzz as they flew overhead and take long naps in the sun on the High Meadow. Edward wondered what it would be like to hike from the High Meadow, across the Great Road and down to Big Pine Lake. He thought, perhaps another adventure for another day.

THE END

Peep
Peep
Peep

# THE SPRING PEEPERS

It had been a long, cold winter on Big Pine Lake. The woodchucks slept soundly in their burrows beneath the High Meadow and J. Duncan Beaver was curled up in his lodge beneath the ice on the North Pond. They all dreamed of the warm sun and the gentle breeze that would melt the ice and bring spring back to Big Pine Lake.

Deep in the mud beneath the shallow marsh of the Bull Frog Bog, Tucker the tree toad was beginning to stir. The warm afternoon sun was melting the frost from the ground and the ice from the lake. As the mud he had slept in all winter began to warm, Tucker stretched his legs and reached up toward the warmth. He grabbed a small willow root and slowly pulled himself out into the bright sunlight.

Tucker climbed higher into the old willow and sat quietly warming himself on a sunny branch. The afternoon sun felt good on his back. He wondered if there were any other tree toads awake yet. First Tucker looked all around. There were still small patches of snow beneath the shaded rocks and fallen trees. He could see that there were no new leaves or patches of soft green carpet moss and there were no butterflies or insects dodging the waving brown marsh grass. Was Tucker too early for spring?

Wondering why everything was so quiet, Tucker would do what all tree toads do on early spring evenings. He would sing and another tree toad would surely answer. As the sun began to set, he climbed out toward the end of the branch, took a deep breath and sang out in his very best spring voice. "Peep-peep peep, peep-peep peep." He stopped to listen, ever so quietly but heard only the sound of the breeze. Again he sang out, "Peep-peep peep, Peep-peep peep. Tucker listened again. Still there was no answer. The Bull Frog Bog was silent.

Slowly he crawled back down the branch. Tucker felt quite alone. He crawled sadly into a small, protected hole in the tree trunk as night fell. Soon it began to rain and a cold wind howled through the branches. He looked out into the night, wishing there was just one small voice on the shore of Big Pine Lake to sing back to him.

The rain turned into big wet snow flakes. Tucker shivered as the wind blew into his hole and the snow began to pile up on the branches of the creeking weeping willow tree. It felt like winter again.

The next morning came with no sun. The gray sky and the new snow covered the Bull Frog Bog, the Quiet Cove and the Beaver Dam. Ice had frozen over Tuckers hole in the tree. He was wet, cold and very lonely.

The sun finally melted the ice on the second day. Tucker pulled himself up to the edge of the hole as night fell again. Would anyone hear him tonight? Once again, into the dark evening sky, he sang out. Peep-peep peep, Peep-peep peep. The snow muffled his song and once again there was no answer. Again and again, he sang out, only to hear the lonely howl of the wind. Tears formed in Tucker's eyes as he sank back into the hole in the tree trunk. Where were the other Peepers?

Three days and three long nights passed. Then on the fourth day, a warm sun came with the morning. Tucker heard the melting snow dripping from the branches into puddles beneath the willow tree. Just maybe, Tucker would hear an answer tonight.

He watched carefully all day for signs of life. He saw Dred the Red Fox at the edge of the Quiet Cove. The foxes were hungry too. One lone robin , looking for worms, picked at the ground and Roger the fish eagle soared high above in search of open water and fresh fish.

As evening approached and the sun began to set, Tucker ventured out onto the branch one more time. He cleared his throat "a-hum, a-hum" and sang out into the evening silence." Peep-peep peep, Peep-peep peep." Again he listened carefully. Again and again he sang out, "Peep-peep Peep-peep peep.

Tucker had nearly given up but he knew that he had just one more call in his tired throat. "A-hum, a-hum" he cleared his throat one more time and sang out in his finest spring voice. "Peep-peep peep! Peep-peep peep"!

Then, far in the distance in the direction of the Quiet Cove, came the most beautiful sound Tucker had ever heard. "Peep Peep-peep, Peep Peep-peep"! It was the song of another spring peeper tree toad singing into the evening sky. Tucker's heart jumped for joy!

He scrambled down the trunk of the willow tree and hopped as fast as he could in the direction of the song ringing in the distance. As he reached the base of an old shag bark hickory tree, he looked up into the dark branches. Just above him, there, on a small branch sat Dinah, singing her own song into the night sky. Peep Peep-peep, Peep peep-peep" Tucker climbed up to Dinah's branch, introduced himself and smiled a very wide smile. Together, they sang into the night sky. Peep-peep-peep, Peep- peep-peep.

Now, as the weather warms and the skies fade into evening dusk, the Bull Frog Bog and the Quiet Cove ring out with the songs of hundreds of spring peepers. Their songs fill the night sky once again and early in the spring, if you're very quiet, listen into the evening woods and you too might hear them sing in their finest voices ever. "Peep-peep-peep. Peep- peep -peep.

THE END

Whoosh!

# THE WHOOSH!

Edward and Uncle Bert sat quietly on the edge of the High Meadow, peering through the tall grass. The Great Road passed far below, marked by the long yellow lines down its middle. It stretched as far as the eye could see, around the wide curve and on toward Hazardville but the woodchucks on the High Meadow could not see the cars and trucks as they passed by. They could only hear the sound. Whoosh! Whoosh.........Whoosh!

The sound of the Whoosh made Uncle Bert wary. His old friend Thayer had gone down to the Great Road yesterday morning and had not returned. If he hadn't looked carefully in both directions before he crossed the road, he could have been run over by the Whoosh, a terrible fate indeed.

Edward had no idea what a Whoosh was. He had heard the sound but had never seen one up close. He could see that Uncle Bert was very upset but Edward was very curious. "Exactly what is a Whoosh, Uncle Bert?" Edward wanted to know. Uncle Bert thought for a minute, wrinkling his nose and smoothing his whiskers with his paw. He couldn't exactly describe the Whoosh. It just had to be seen.

So, Edward and Uncle Bert set off down the clearly marked trail in search of the Whoosh. They passed their burrows, the Look-Out Rock and the endless field of sweet red clover. When they came near the Great Road, Uncle Bert found a tall climbing rock that poked up just higher than the grass that waved in the wind.

"Climb up, Edward." Uncle Bert said. " From here you should be able to clearly see the Whoosh." Edward climbed up, stretching his short legs as far as he could, to reach the top of the rock. He sat down beside Uncle Bert, balancing with his tail to watch for the Whoosh. They sat for what seemed to be a very long time, both dozing a little in the warm sun. Then, from out of nowhere.........came a Whoosh!

Edward and Uncle Bert jumped with surprise! They looked in the direction of the sound but saw only the tall grass. The Whoosh had disappeared. Once again they dozed off in the warm sun. WHOOSH! WHOOSH! Again they jumped up! This time they landed on top of each other, arms and legs swinging everywhere. Uncle Bert looked one way and Edward looked the other. Still they saw nothing but the tops of the tall grass, waving in the wind.

"We must get closer', said Uncle Bert. "We need to see the Whoosh quickly before it disappears." They climbed down from the rock and crawled, ever so carefully through the tall grass, toward the very edge of the Great Road. Uncle Bert thought about his old friend Thayer and Edward thought about lunch, which he had missed.

As they neared the edge of the Great Road, they could

hear the sounds more clearly. Whoosh!......Whoosh!...... Whoosh! Without thinking, Edward stepped out of the weeds in the direction of the sound, right onto the edge of the Great Road. Uncle Bert caught him by the end of his tail and with a mighty tug, pulled him sprawling back into the weeds, just as another Whoosh whizzed by.

"What was that?" cried Edward. "That, young man was a Thundering Yellow Whoosh and if you don't learn quickly, you'll end up under its wheels like my old friend Thayer. The Great Road is a very dangerous place and you must learn to listen carefully and look both ways before you try to cross. Let me show you how."

"First you perk your ears up and listen carefully. Then you look both ways to be sure there are no Whooshes coming from either direction. Watch me." Edward watched carefully as Uncle Bert stepped slowly through the opening in the weeds at the edge of the road. He had never seen Uncle Bert be so careful but after being scared nearly to death by the Thundering Yellow Whoosh, he was beginning to understand.

Uncle Bert first perked his ears up, stood very still and listened carefully He heard the breeze moving through the pine trees and the rustling of the striped skunk digging his hole. He even heard the tic-tic- ticking of the tiny woodpecker on the old dead pine tree but he didn't hear a Whoosh. Then ever so carefully, he took one step beyond the tall grass, leaned cautiously forward and turned his head first to the left and then to the right, looking as far as he could see in both directions.

Edward, still trembling from the scare of the

Thundering Yellow Whoosh, peered out from the narrow break in the tall grass. He stepped one timid foot onto the Great Road, perked his ears up and listened. He too could hear the wind in the pine trees, the rustling of the striped skunk and the tic-tic-ticking of the tiny woodpecker but when he looked to the left he saw a Bright Red Whoosh, whizzing toward them.!

Uncle Bert saw it at the same time and together they jumped back to the safety of the tall grass as the Bright Red Whoosh zoomed by. "I saw one Uncle Bert! It was a Bright RED Whoosh! It has shiny chrome bumpers and bright red paint and black tires that spin as it whizzes by. It is SO BIG and we are so small that it can't see us. Now I know why we have to be so careful before we walk into the road."

Uncle Bert had nearly all the excitement he could handle for one day and Edward was listening to his stomach make noises because he was still very hungry so they decided to search for some sweet blue berries and get away from the Great Road and the sound of the Whoosh. On their way back to the clearly marked trail, Uncle Bert stopped suddenly. He perked his little ears up and listened carefully. "Do you hear that Edward? It's the sound of chewing and the smell of ripe blue berries. It's coming from over near that clearing." Edward listened carefully. Sure enough, he could hear the munch, munch munching and he could smell the ripe berries too. Ever so slowly, Edward and Uncle Bert crept toward the sound.

When they knew they were close to the sound, Uncle Bert poked his nose carefully through the tall grass into the clearing beside the clearly marked trail. He jumped into the air shouting WHOOPIE!! Edward just stood there amazed. Sitting there in the clearing, beside a basket of fresh, ripe blue berries was Thayer, all safe and sound.

Uncle Bert jumped up and down and hugged Thayer and talked very fast about the Whooshes and the Great Road and looking both ways and how afraid he had been that Thayer had been run over and squashed by the Whoosh. Edward was mostly concerned with the fact that he had missed lunch and sat down beside the basket of fresh berries, hoping that Thayer would be willing to share.

After supper, Uncle Bert, Thayer and Edward climbed back up the clearly marked trail to the High Meadow. Uncle Bert and Thayer sat on the Look-Out Rock to talk while Edward curled up in his burrow on his bed of soft marsh hay. He dreamed of the adventure on the Great Road, about the Thundering Red Whoosh, the sweet blue berry lunch and finding Thayer all safe and sound. Then Uncle Bert and Thayer crawled into their burrows and fell fast asleep.

THE END